Today I feel sad.
My face wears a frown.

I'm slumping, and slouching,
and feeling quite down.

The sky is all gray,
and it's raining outside.

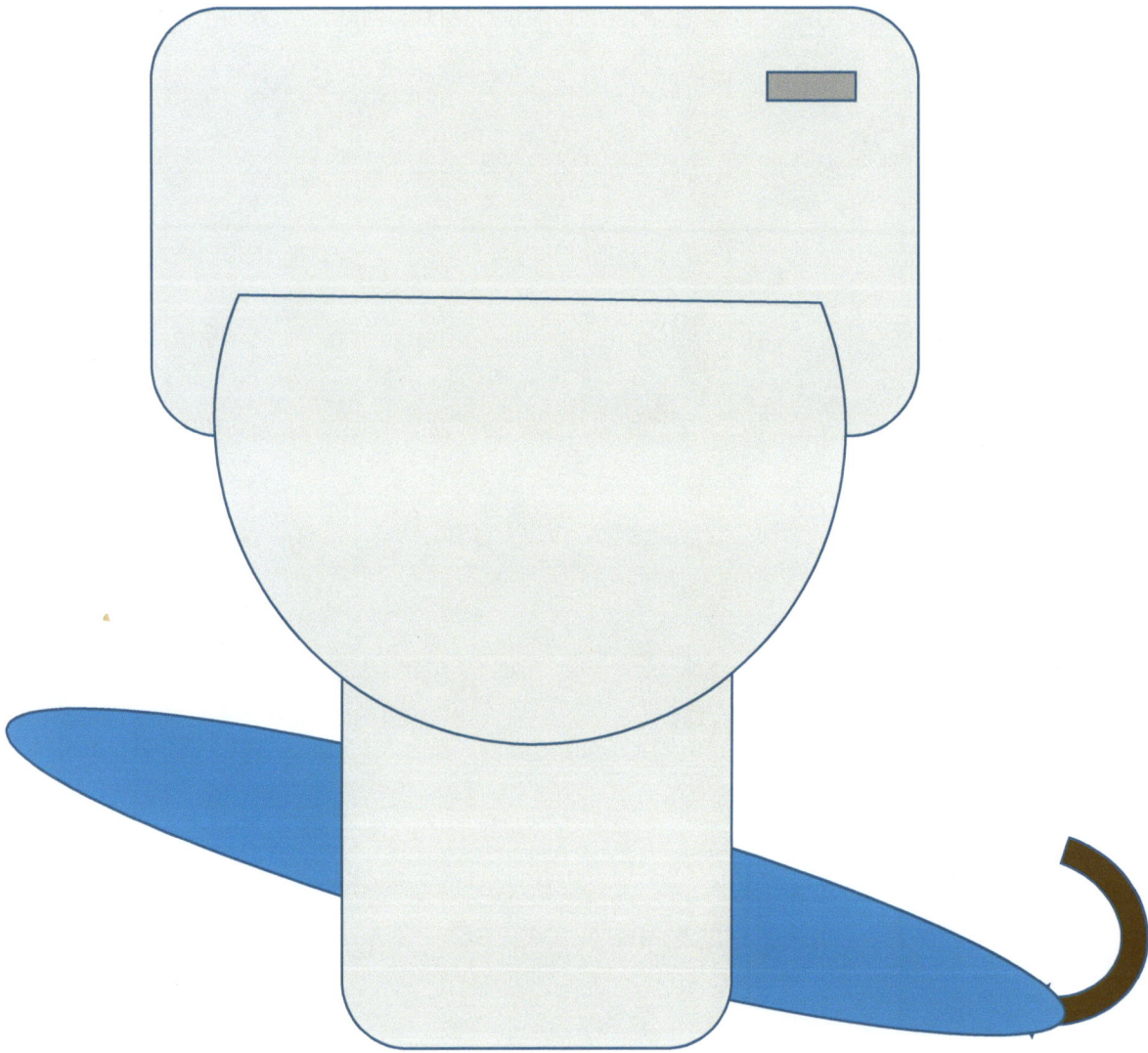

I can't find my umbrella.
Where would it hide?

I step in a puddle.
My hair is all wet.

By the time I'm at school
it is not quite dry, yet.

My glue stick is empty.
My crayons are all broken.

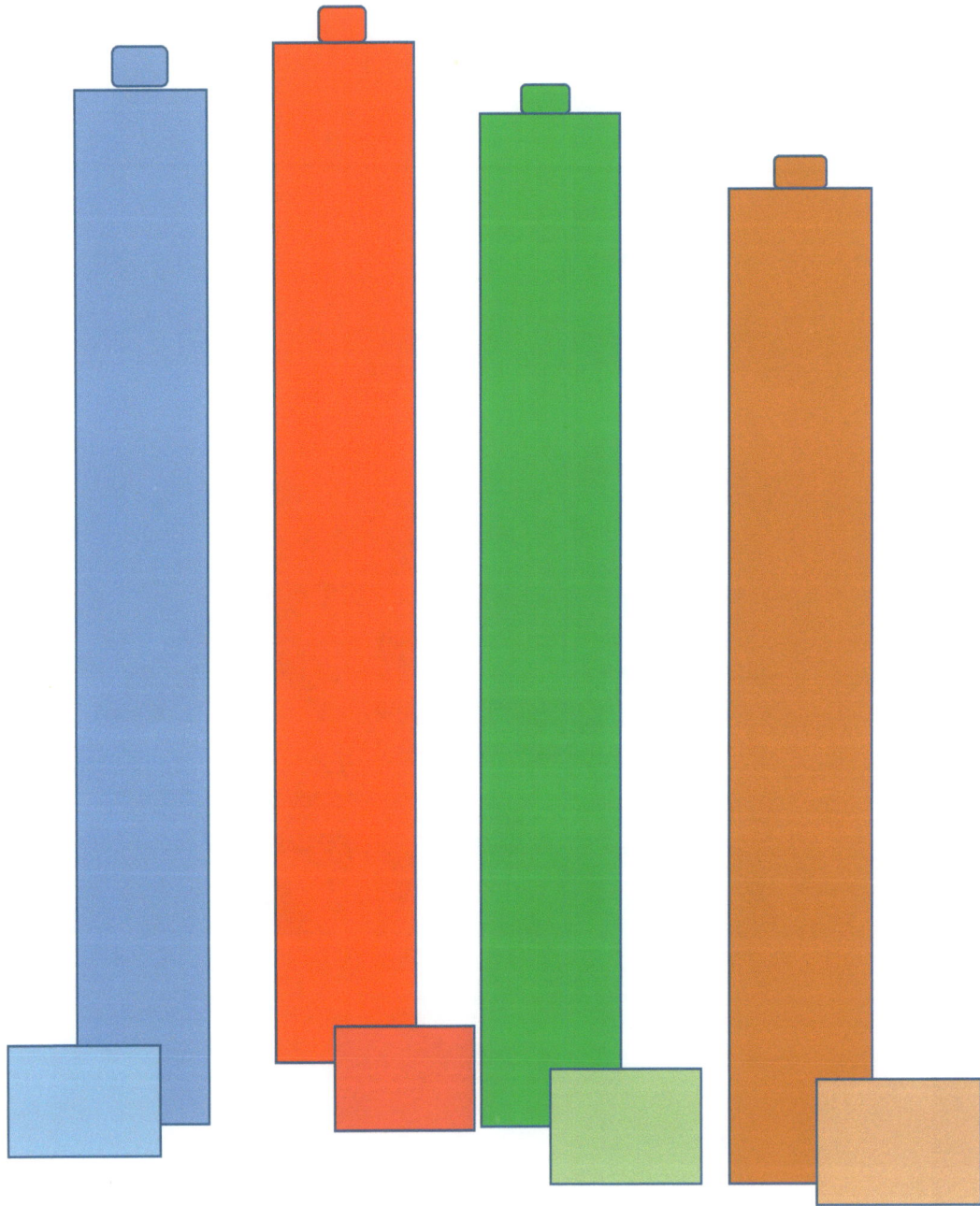

My markers are dried up.
You've got to be jokin'!

When we play in the gym,
I'm not picked for the game.

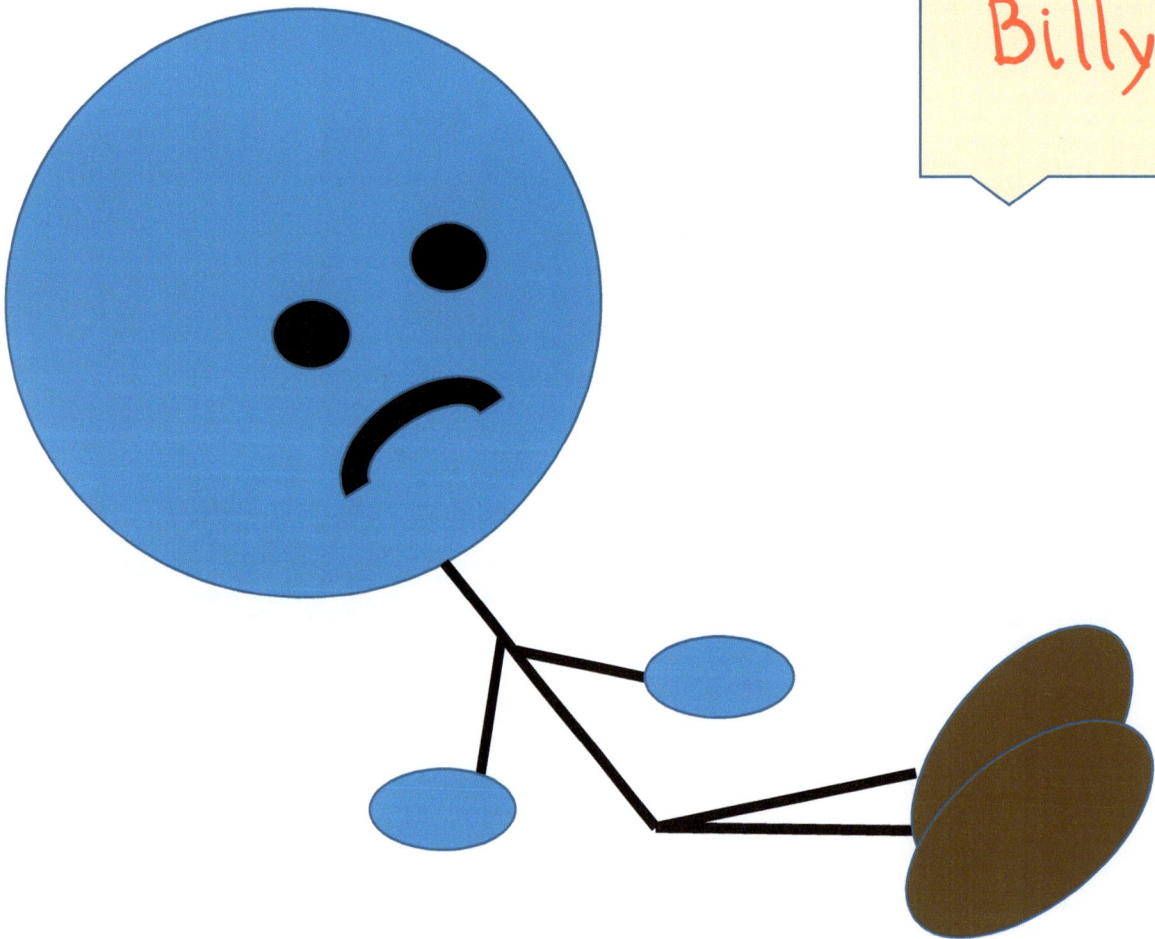

I wait and I wait,
but I don't hear my name.

So I sigh and I slouch,
put my head on the table.

I try hard to smile,
but I just am not able.

My friend tells me, "NO!"
this is _her_ place in line.

1, 2, 3,
4, 5,
7, 8,
9,
6

In math I forget
where to write 6 and 9.

When I get home,
I can't find my favorite toy.

I search and I search,
'til my room I destroy.

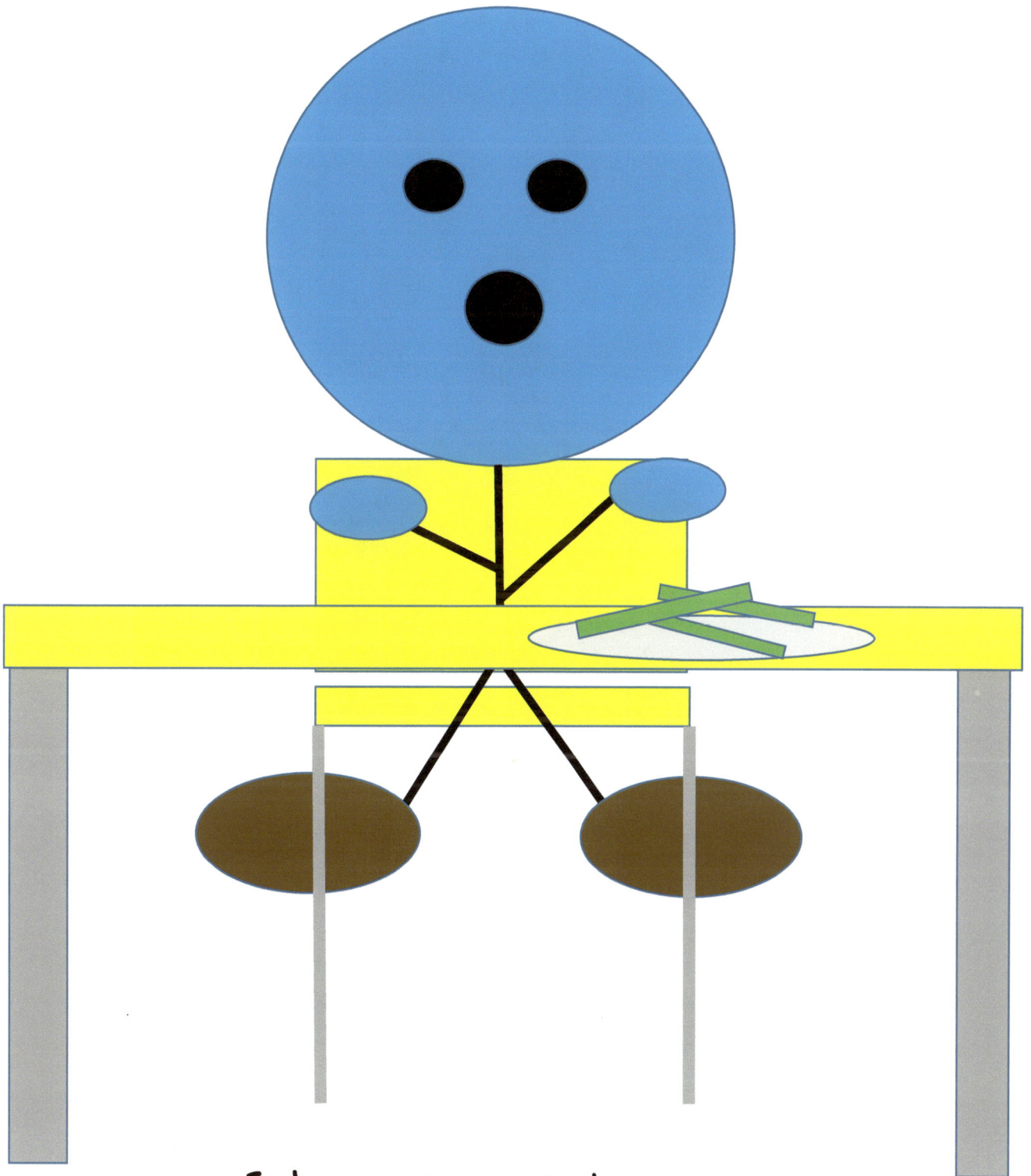

I have to eat beans.
"I don't want to!" I blurt.

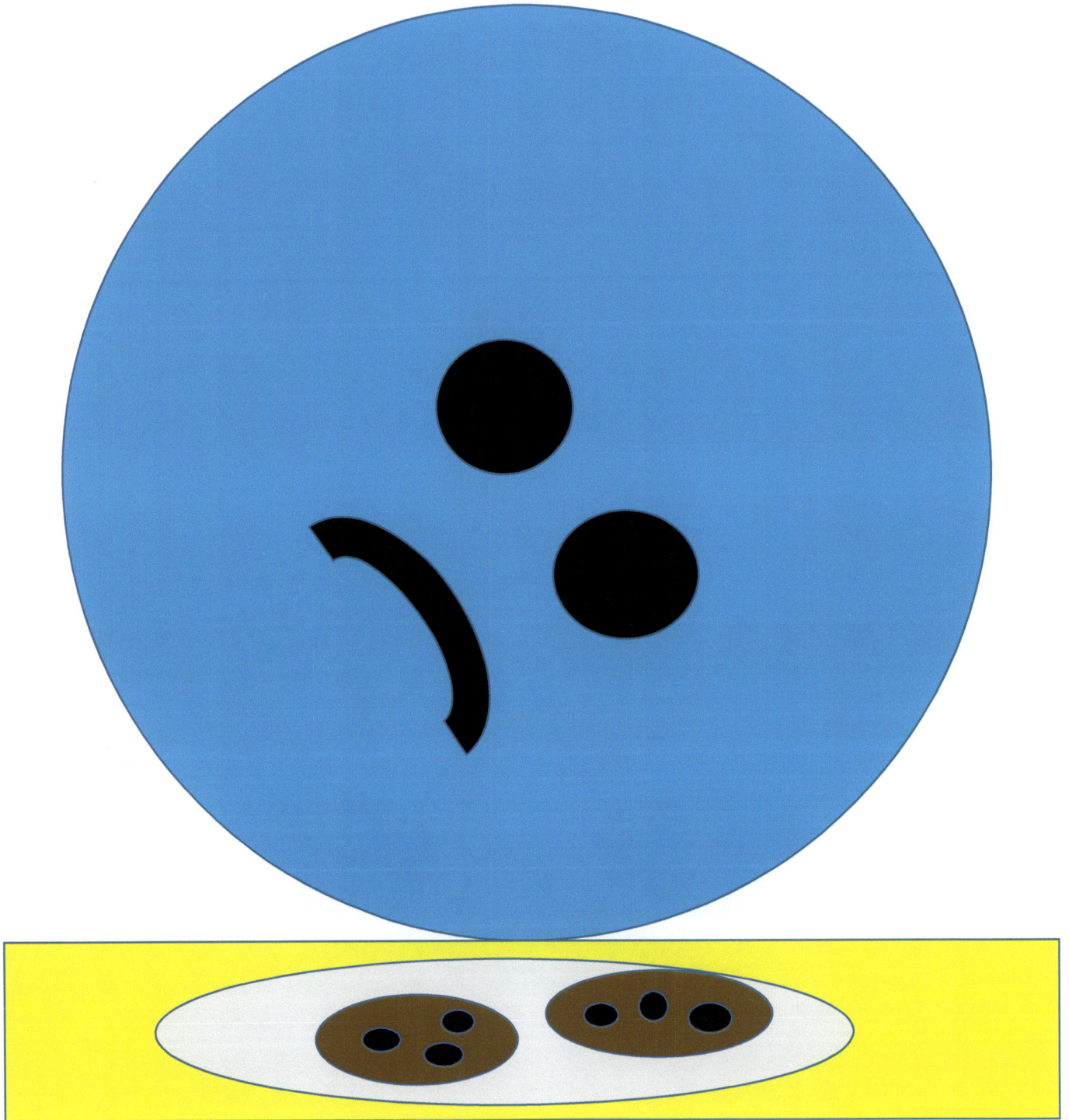

So mom says
I don't get to eat my dessert.

My nose starts to sniffle.
My lips start to pout.

My eyes start to water,
tears begin to fall out.

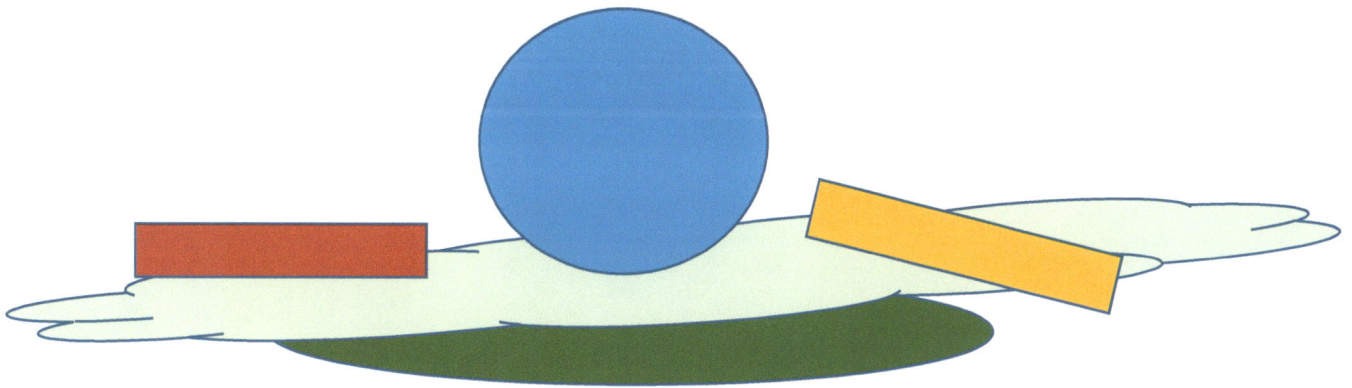

My pillow is missing,
it seems to be lost(ed).

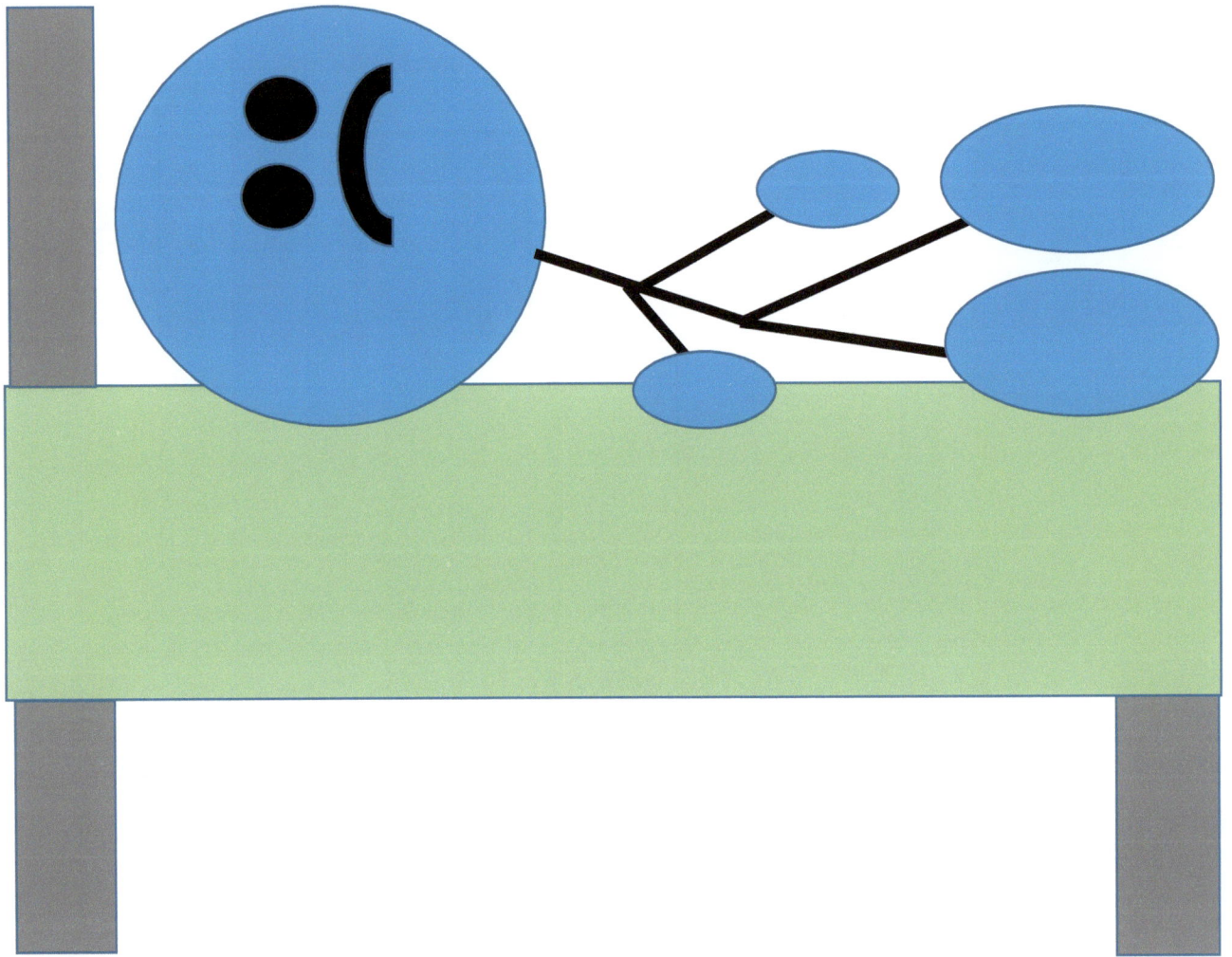

I lie down without it,
because I'm exhausted.

Z Z z z z

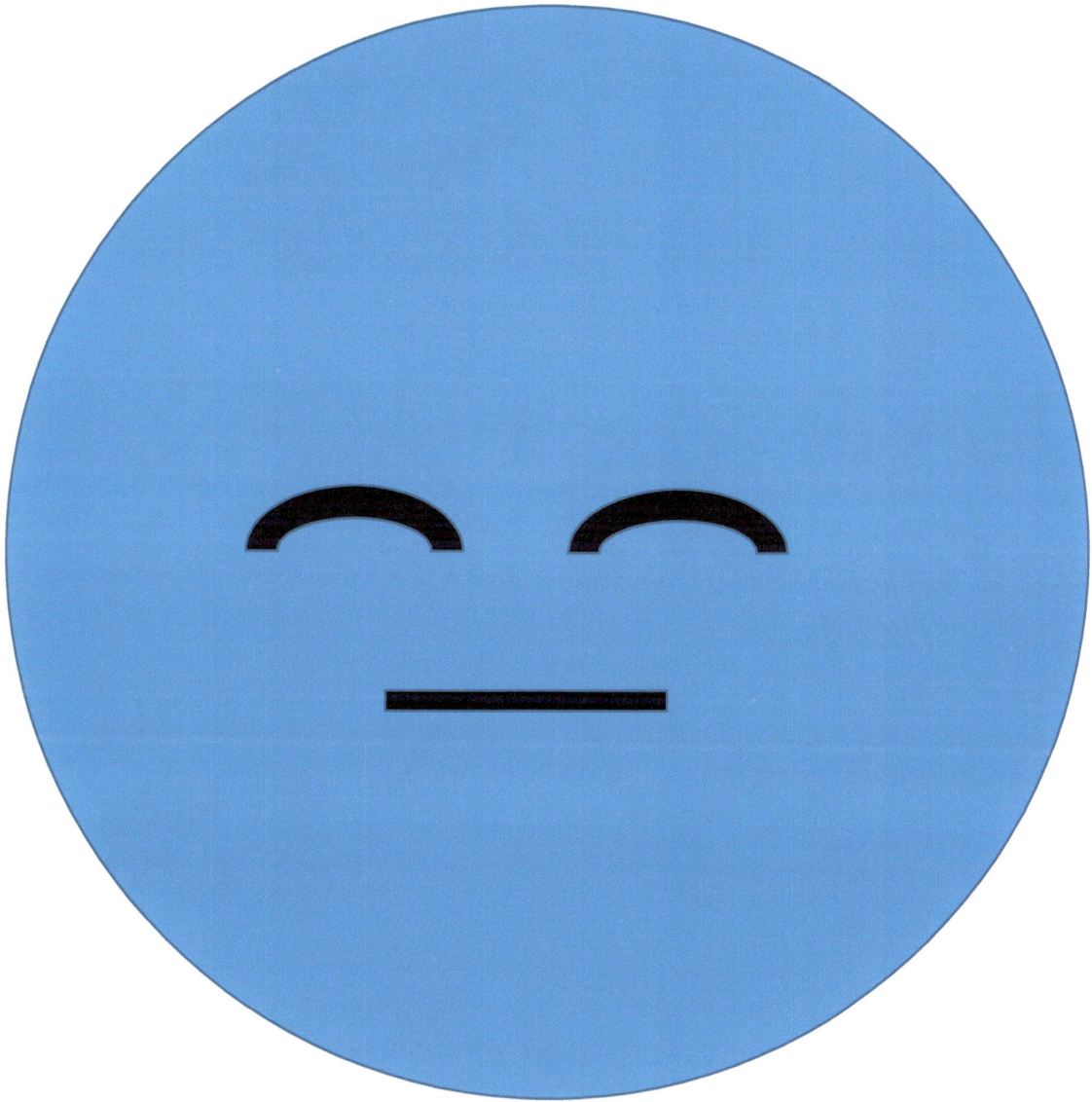

I drift off to sleep,
what a bad day I've had!

Tomorrow will be better,
but today I felt sad.

Name _____

Draw a picture of what makes you sad.

Name _____

Draw a picture of your favorite toy.

Name _____

Draw a picture of what makes you sad.

I am sad when _____

_____

_____.

Name _____

Draw a picture of your favorite toy.

My favorite toy is my

Name _____

Draw a picture of how you would make someone happy.

I would make someone

happy by _____

_____

_____.